First, Do No Harm

Also by Laura Brylawski-Miller

Poetry

Luna Parks

The Snow on Lake Como

Exile at Sarzana

Fiction

The Square at Vigevano

The Medusa's Smile

The Shadow of the Evening

(L'Ombra della Sera)

First, Do No Harm
NEW AND SELECTED POEMS

Laura Brylawski-Miller

Poets' Choice Publishing

Copyright © 2017 Poets' Choice Publishing
All rights reserved
Printed in the United States of America

Cover art by Micheline Klagsbrun
"Spindrift 2," ink on vellum, 36" x 98"
For more information: www.michelineklagsbrun.com

Consultant work:
www.WilliamMeredithFoundation.org

Bulk discounts available through www.Poets-Choice.com

Library of Congress Cataloging-in-Publication Data pending
ISBN 978-0-9972629-5-7

Poets' Choice

Poets' Choice Publishing
337 Kitemaug Road
Uncasville, CT 06382
Poets-Choice.com

*To the past,
with gratitude*

ACKNOWLEDGMENT

Since I tend not to submit individual poems for publication, the poems in the first section of this collection have not yet appeared in print. They have not been held in a vacuum, though—on the contrary, they have been discussed, analyzed and, when needed, vivisected in monthly workshop sessions at a Chinese restaurant with fellow poets Patricia Garfinkel, Michael Davis and Kathi Wolfe. I am indebted to them for the insights, support and needed pointing out of my occasionally idiosyncratic syntax. Evenings of friends and poetry, with wisdom from Chinese cookies. Bliss, indeed.

A grateful thank you also to Sid Gold for his advice in the selection of the poems, for suggesting Richard Harteis as a publisher, and for all his help, past and present, with my manuscripts.

CONTENTS

Introduction xi

SEASONS
Beach on the Bay 3
Japanese Woodcut 4
Green Elegy 5
Sunday in August 6
The Cats at Ephesus 7
March 15 8
Versilia 9
Grey Elegy—Cape May 11
Spring 12
November 13
Déjeuner Sur L'herbe 14
Downhill Racer 15
Autumn 16
February 17
Snow Elegy 18

BOTANY
Brendan's Cyclamen 21
Driving to Lübeck 22
Magnolia in a Georgetown Garden 23
Wild Flowers 24
Crossing the Border 26
Bignonias 28

FOOLS AND LOVERS

Concierto de Aranjuez 31
My Modigliani 32
Metamorphosis 33
Letter from Hell 34
Gone 35
Words 36
Portrait 37
The Pearl Fishers—Bizet 38
Sketchbook 39
The Golden Touch 40
Transgressions 41
Panta Rhei? 42
Ay, Que Trabajo Me Questa 43
360 45
Cherrydale Flea Market 46
The Beginning 47
Ballad of Other Times 48
Shortcuts 50
Touch 51
Walking in Milan 52

Selections from *The Snow on Lake Como*

Graffiti at the Como Railroad Station 57
Nostalgia Latina 60
Evening of the Fiesta 61
Cabo de las Huertas 62
September Morning at the Lido 64
Venice Under the Snow 65

Airport Highway, New Orleans   66
Things I Learned in Surgery   67
Moonlight   68
The Ambush   69
Looking Back   70
Driving to an Unknown Place for the Weekend   71
The Square at Vigevano   72
Advent   77
Kalevala   78
The Horn of Roland   79
Galatea   81
Eurydice   82
Cygnet   83
The Prodigal Son   84
Tapestry   85
The Snow on Lake Como   86

Selections from *Exile at Sarzana*

"Like Snow on a Windless Alp"   93
Volterra   94
Street Musicians, Lucca   97
Meson del Coso   98
End of Day   100
Fishtail Lodge, Pokhara   101
Sky Burial   102
The Castle   103
Castles in Air   105
The Inmates   106
Pavane for a Dead Princess   107
The Stars of the Bear   108

The King of a Rainy Country   110
Fog   112
Via Cerva   113
March Storm   115
Thinking of You on a March Morning   116
Three Chinese Poems   117
Winters   119
Elegy   120
Blue Elegy   121
Marrons Glacés   122
Luna Parks   124
Fly Fishing—Lake Como   127
Mallorquin   129
Monterosso   130
Scuba   132
Ocean City   134
Memorial Day, Cape May, 2007   137
The Shape of Water   139
Kismet   140
Of Saints and Snows   141
Going Back   143
Letter to Yang Chen Chai   144
Opera Ball at the German Embassy   145

About the Author   149

INTRODUCTION

By Richard Harteis

In Robert Fagles' translation of Vergil, Aeneas, contemplating the Trojan War cries out, "The world is a world of tears, and the burdens of mortality touch the heart." Laura Brylawski-Miller intuits the lacrimae rerum, the tears in things throughout her poetry, and it is not only a result of the classic education she received in her native Italy, but a guiding insight that directs her view of the world, the shape of her soul. Like the Buddha of Sokkuram, she is stunned by the suffering she sees in the world and is left with the only possible response, compassion for the human condition. Compassion in her, however, is not naiveté. This intuition is perhaps what first led her to medicine, the sensitivity for the pain of others, the need to heal, even when that healing process means debriding dead tissue with her poetic scalpel. "First, do no harm," the Hippocratic oath demands, but sometimes it requires severe measures as every surgeon knows.

Laura has a house in Bellagio, that lake-view village where Pliny the Younger retreated from the summer's heat in Rome. There, when autumn seeps into the hills about Lake Como, the air is filled with the sweet smell of burning leaves, smoke rising like the vapors about the oracle in Delphi recalling the weight of time, the precious brevity of life. Like a soothsayer, or shaman, she intuits nature as it interacts with human consciousness, a literary device critics call pathetic fal-lacy, ascribing human sensibilities to nonhuman objects in nature: in her poems, the sun "bleeds on the horizon," "the new-born sea breathes quietly," the seaweed "holds winter's spent fury in long green fingers." Like the imagist poet Paul Valéry she knows that poems are not made of ideas, but of images and this philosophy is only ever evident in her poetry in practice, not theory. It reveals the synchronicity of physical fact and spiritual reality. Mind and body be-come one, interacting with and creating the world at once, the method of magic. Yet these poems are as real, as accessible as the air we breathe, or the pain one feels at an injury. In their mild way, they are heart-breaking. She is both down-to-earth and a marvel. Laura's working method is invariably the same in all the poems, a pattern she has developed to perfection. Only after she has set the scene with precise images does she startle the reader with an unexpected epiphany. For Peter Meinke, for example, her poem, "Green Elegy" offers "not hope, exactly, but affection, mercy, and ordinary kindness." But the charming image of a tiny rabbit taking refuge in the hospice park is undercut by the final chilling observation that the tiny rabbit, "doesn't know dogs come here to play."

It is our good fortune to be able to share her work with you, a book we hope you will wish to return to time and time again for the pleasure that good poetry can provide in a world sorely in need of such beauty as it is at present.

I

Seasons

BEACH ON THE BAY

Fragments of jellyfish
imprison water,
a crab scuttles away.
A silent, unkempt beach
that only nature litters:
grey skeletons of trees
emerge from sand,
pale broken shells,
the empty armor
of horseshoe crabs.
Tangled sea grass—
a hint of jungle
turns a footprint
into a discovery.
In red-striped chairs
two middle-aged men
lie naked in the sun,
decaying bronze statues
betrayed by time.

JAPANESE WOODCUT, 1920

Hasui Kawase

Evening snow
falls on Terajima village—
flat, secret houses beckon
with yellow-
lit windows,
white bridges
span a ribbon
of solitary water.
The man walks uphill
alone in white silence—
black clothes,
black poles like black
signposts along a road
as yet unknown:
the earthquake will come
and Hiroshima
will flame those windows
but on this evening
snow descends
in lonely innocence.

GREEN ELEGY

August, heat flows
into bones white
as the waiting snows,
the sun bleeds
at the horizon
and summer flames
unaware it's dying.
But the swallows know
and we do too. Still
green offers shady
comfort to the tiny
rabbit at breakfast in
the hospice park.
He doesn't know dogs
come here to play.

SUNDAY IN AUGUST

Three sparrows
frolic in a lot's dust
like children at the pool.
An empty ribbon of sidewalk,
no passing cars. A day
held on a cusp of silence as on
the edge of an adventure one
might regret. Heat
sucks the bones of will,
empties the mind.
But the skin in the sun knows
the sparrows' pleasure.

THE CATS AT EPHESUS

They lounge on broken columns
make statues of themselves
as we swarm among the ruins—
motley, clueless invaders
a guide up-raised umbrella
our wayward standard.
We look and listen,
take pictures of each other against
pediments, seek connections to a
past not ours own. We are aliens
here, loud and blind: we'll never
know Antinoos' beauty, nor
Hadrian's cosmic grief, nor that
pristine, lapis sea. So we trudge on
aimless under the Turkish sun
guzzling water, leave plastic bottles
as our spoor. From their columns
the cats watch us go by
with timeless eyes. If
caressed, they nod,
accept our tribute
with regal condescension.
An homage owed, pleasant
and ephemeral—irrelevant
as our presence here.

MARCH 15

The dying peach tree
by the hospice door
is blooming crimson:
a last surge of blood
in blackened branches,
defiant cry
for life betrayed
by an end
out of season.

In the greening park
an unseen dove
mourns "*et tu, et tu.*"
It is the Ides
of March. Beware.

VERSILIA

(Tuscany)

Summer of a silent hawk
high-wheeling over pines
where the wind from the sea
would lose its way, whispers
of insects in the reeds
along the drowsy river. Layered
heat of early afternoon,
the world asleep. We stood
in the path's glaucous shade,
awkward adolescent silence
between us. Your hands,
too big for your wrists
tormenting a leaf. A gangly boy,
too poor and homely
for me. "Girls like you
don't know," you said. Blue
eyes, as blue as the Tyrrhenian
sea. "You'll get over it" I said.
I didn't want to see your eyes.

But, Delio, even girls like me
come to know. The wounds
of loving wrong, the careless
ambush from blade-words,
the stony, useless taste
of regret. Last year,
driving back here
to Versilia, I saw again the pines
and near the sea, the fields
red with poppies, a quiet bleeding

under the rain. So many years
since that summer. And you
came back, Delio.
I owed you this.

GREY ELEGY—CAPE MAY

The sea stormed last night
but now lies still, somber
and silent as a winter lake.
A forecast of snow whitens
the air, erases memories
of summer. On the beach
a runner parts the mist
as he hurries to nowhere—
past and future flow by
in his steps. We're transients
here, and *scire nefas*. But there is
grey comfort in the unknown.

SPRING

Panhandlers
are suddenly in bloom
at every corner, turn stop signs
into gauntlets. I give
to the old ones: victims or cons
what does it matter now,
at journey's end? The young man
holding up a cardboard saga, his
girlfriend sunbathing nearby,
stem empathy: they look healthy
and are smoking. Still,
I pull away conflicted—why
judge an unknown story?
At the next traffic light
an ancient reprobate winks at me
as he takes my money, restores
the balance. Enjoy that beer,
Grandpa. April is finally here.

NOVEMBER

Fog blankets the Potomac
this morning, another grey
amorphous river meanders
above denuded trees,
evokes ghosts. Peaceful ones,
like faded photographs,
a silent movie of memories
softened by mist, passions and
mistakes now equally precious,
equally owned.

I love the way this fog
lets me forgive myself
for what I can't change,
brings freedom to recall
a taste of salt on skin
in blue summers, the naïve
disbeliefs of gone springs.
Now in November the trees
emerge naked from the fog,
unmask to skeletal frames.
December snow will soften
the lost fallen leaves.

DÉJEUNER SUR L'HERBE

Dandelion vests
shed like alien skins
on the cool grass,
construction workers
from the hi-rise
lunch on the lawn
of the garden apartments
across the street.
Soft Latin vowels.
One stretches out
in the blue shade.
Siesta time in a village
transplanted, a moment
of oblivion. The grey
cement sidewalk
on Wilson Boulevard
has become Lethe.

DOWNHILL RACER

Your life, if it stood still enough
to be painted, would be a landscape by
Vlaminck: fugitive houses
along a fleeting road, or even more,
the quick eye of the camera
strapped to the Olympic skier—
a dizzying blur where only
the goal is clear. Not a race
pour le sport—gold medals
don't come that way. Triumph
demands the unswerving eye
of perfect timing, fine-honed need
to be the best. I understand.
But, will you ever miss the
fascination of dead ends,
mistakes that lead
to uncharted, useless discoveries,
wrong but unforgotten loves?
In the surge of the crowd at the
finish, the TV, the microphones, the
cheers will you look back at me—
who wandered off at the first turn—
sunbathing on the hill,
gathering wild strawberries
in the snow?

AUTUMN

The wind beats the lake tonight
and splits the currents into a crash
of waves—warring discordant cymbals,
a metronomic heartbeat denatured
into uncertainties. The hard, cold sky,
is swept in an ambush of frozen stars.
September dies in the first yellow leaves
of the fig tree. You think of all
the wrong directions taken,
what could have made a difference.

FEBRUARY

You crossed the dark street,
entered the lobby, turned.
For a moment, framed
in light and glass,
you seemed arrested
in time, forever
secluded, walled in ice
like a Norse warrior.
Then you raised a hand,
waved, walked in. Away
from the light, away
to an unknown place
shared only in memory.

SNOW ELEGY

The snows
of yesterday
have lost
their innocence,
turned
into grimy mounds
that pee dejected
on dirty sidewalks.
A few ice crystals
still sparkle
valiant and doomed
in the spring-like sun.
We soil everything.

II

Botany

BRENDAN'S CYCLAMEN
1/1/2007

It came the day you died.
January blossoms, snowy
hothouse cousins of the wild
small crimson ones I used to pick
on faraway mountains, long ago.
That first winter,
those ever-blooming flowers
became your presence,
something to hold on to.
By summer, out on the terrace with
the orchids, it must have yearned
for the woods, shriveled down to
flaccid misshaped leaves sagging in
the sun and risked the trashcan. By
late fall it revived, a few puny,
wintry petals emerged, wan ghosts
of memories time might take away.

But how long can one ask a bulb
to bloom? After seven years
this seemed the summer to let go:
two yellow leaves, drooping depleted
over the clay rim. Still, we couldn't do it.
And now in January, fifteen, no, seventeen
long stems are lifting a graceful cobra's head
over the dark jade leaves—pointy
inquisitive buds begin to unfurl. One
for each of your years. White as January
snow, white as a page left unwritten,
white as hope and grief.

DRIVING TO LÜBECK

June's wildflowers
can't tell borders:
they strayed, riotous and free
through no-man's land, heedless
of warning as they crossed
the bloody rent in a divided heart.
"People died here, trying
to escape" our East German guide
tells us. She knows events
but is too young to know
how it felt, your own country
a prison. Today only a sign
tells the story, muted grey
by the side of the highway.
The cold Baltic wind comes in
to shake it, ruffles the daisies
by the sign's feet, goes on
with us toward Lübeck.
The wind, too, cannot read.

MAGNOLIA IN A GEORGETOWN GARDEN

Grandiflora,
petals of white jade
snowy Turandot
guarded by armored
enameled leaves
cool moonflower
in a cave of shade
untouched aloof
while July flames
the brick sidewalk
sears the wan grass
shrivels innocent
petunias by the steps.

Yet if touched
you wither.

WILD FLOWERS

Listen, a rose
always gets poems
and Cynara's pale lilies
bloom on, un-faded on Victorian
pages. But, for me, give me wild
flowers in the city. A torn-down
building's seedy lot, concrete remnants
of abandoned lives
blurred by fringed unruly green:
dandelions, poking scruffy heads
through a chain-link fence
(curious children penned in a school
yard) uncouth thistle, blushing clover
or those unnamed cerulean stars
ethereal on rough stems
I knew in another continent,
fellow travelers to an alien shore.

Wild flowers need no passport, defy
place and time on stubborn roots,
invade centuries unscathed.

Dürer's etched bignonia
spills in flaming trumpets
on a retaining wall by the canal,
airy summer snowflakes
of Queen Anne's lace
behind the Exxon station
sway in the wind

like dancing ladies at the court.
Yes, a rose is a rose,
but give me that stop sign
where a crack in the pavement
has grown a perfect daisy. Life
recurrent sweetens our finite one.

CROSSING THE BORDER

Dandelions riot
on the escarpment
by the Central Library—
below the tennis fence
a ditch has filled
with yesterday's rain.
The softened air
brings back lost springs,
mutates these yellow
disheveled commoners
into ghostly primroses
along secluded streams.

The past flows in
then ebbs into the shadow
of its essence. Still,
it is a cherished cage
where you hold secrets
polished by time, days
compressed into diamonds
smuggled across the border,
the exile's last hope
sewn into a tattered coat.

How do you let go, divest
yourself of yourself? Should
you? Still, a tardy spring
is finally here. So, turn
a new face to the wind,
learn from these brashly

exuberant upstarts. They
need no woodland streams
and thrive along a drain
where, duckling-yellow,
a fuzzy tennis ball
bobs in leftover rain.

BIGNONIAS

Dürer etching

Ruins
don't tell history:
the Colosseum's
blind eyes
in a Roman sky,
the golden paintings
of the Louvre
only tell life arrested,
a fly in amber—
beautiful and dead.

History
is the return
of wild bignonias
cascading from a wall,
yellow-crimson trumpets
riotous, unchanged
through the chain of years
as Durer saw them
and the people in Pompei
and surely some doe-eyed
Pharaoh before them.

History is life
recurring.

III

Fools and Lovers

CONCIERTO DE ARANJUEZ

Serendipity. A guitar CD
bought in a Venice church: Vivaldi,
a bittersweet Satie, Villa-Lobos
and then Rodrigo. Suddenly
it was there, the dragon cave
at Porto Cristo, a subterranean lake
black as the Styx and the boat
coming from the darkness, a
pinpoint of light like an apparition
of doom or salvation. Then a guitar,
alone, playing the *adagio*. We are
made of what we forget. The past
comes back, rewrites the story we
think we wrote, changes it,
leaves us to the whims
of its wayward winds.

Music born of a garden and grief,
Guernica still bleeding, a new war
soon to come. How are we
what we are? Guernica pales
into Dresden, flames into Hiroshima.

The garden at Aranjuez lives on,
flowers and singing waters bloom
into an enchantment of resurging
music. An undeserved redemption
comes, forfeited long ago: to have
an inured heart once more broken
and healed by the forgotten
voice of a guitar.

MY MODIGLIANI

That first summer, new bride
bewildered by American suburbia
—Manon lost in the wilds of Louisiana—
I would take the trolley to Georgetown
and wander about the leafy streets
in aimless search of myself
as if old bricks might hold the key,
the *ubi consistam* of the uncharted life
I now faced. Opaque days,
swampy heat layering an air
heavy as dead water, heavy
as a grey knowledge: unlike Manon,
transported for her sins
I owned this.

Then, one afternoon of dismal limbo,
she was there: *La Bourguignonne.*
Sooty black dress, long iconic neck,
misaligned empty eyes lost in a dream
among a store's motley ware: my twin,
displaced as I felt. For sale
like a slave, bartered by the owner to
send her kid to camp. My first glorious
art buy, the manifesto
of a turn on the road. So long
ago. She now lives on my wall,
no longer thought weird,
and much admired. We both
are now. But we both remember.

METAMORPHOSIS

We have defeated
nature's failures.
Pacemakers rein in
unruly hearts, ornery
prostates get cored,
titanium substitutes for bone.
Refitted breed,
we hobble toward death
as to an ever-distant shore.
Shiny hips, knees
upset x-ray machines
at airports. Stents
ream out clogged highways
for our blood. We barter
each other spare parts.

Only the soul escapes,
unfound, un-needed.

LETTER FROM HELL

Those who go to pieces
for *une saison en enfer*
should try walking its street for
years, alone, with no care for
flesh burnt beyond feeling,
dreams smothered in the cradle
by careful hands. It's not a place
to raise a child, or meet a friend
at a café, though hope left at the gate
brings freedom: our soul's black flames
burn unrepentent here, to Lucifer's
dark glory. Each day, Charon's boat
emerges from the mist with fresh recruits.
We greet them, get stark news:
days of ice and fire, the four horsemen
are shattering the promises of heaven.
Here, nothing can change. Our stars
are nailheads, merciless and secure.

P.S. Cerberus was enrolled in the K.9.
I miss him.

GONE

The swallows, black-white darts
across the picture window
have gone somewhere,
no longer scissor
the blue evening air
in aerial ballets. The bats, too
have fluttered away.
Even the lizards
scurrying at noon on sunny rocks,
(they leave a wriggling tail
in your hand, if you try to catch them)
are few this year. Russian crows now
roost on the weeping beech, squawk
barbaric challenges to local gulls.

The lake glitters, splendid and unchanged.

So many people died in the village
this past winter, the greengrocer tells me
as we inspect tomatoes. Cancer
in the air, he says. We are all pilgrims,
going unknowing on an unknown road.

The image in my mirror turns opaque.
Men no longer turn when I walk by.
The bangle you clasped on my young skin
will gleam on unchanging, become
an artifact, hawked by auctioneers
some rainy afternoon. Going, going, gone.
Yet, are the swallows, the bats,
even those tailless lizards really gone
when they go on dancing in a poem?

WORDS

The first time I read *Paradise Lost*
I thought of a cathedral built of words,
flying buttresses of angels, falling
fallen ones, a gravity-defying paradox,
foundations hanging in mid air
in a ludicrous, triumphant feat.
Stone words, impervious
to winds and the famished rain,
as Horace boasted in his "*Exegi
monumentum...*" though that too
might have been a conceit—
who remembers him, really,
except for *carpe diem*?

What wonder words are. Loose
change, pennies worn
from too much circulation,
tired doxies pounding
hackneyed streets. Yet
they can own you, make you
forget things, head in the cloud,
even miss the bus as you chase
inside rhymes. Words, and you see
impossible cathedrals in mid-air
some quiet morning as you sit
transfixed at a computer. Outside
indifferent cars go by. A world
lost and regained while Lucifer
plummets howling through eternity
in his magnificent, never-ending fall.

PORTRAIT

Talisman of a smile,
flash of sun on a winter sea,
badly askew, half-closed door
to a secret garden. A snowy city
flat gray against the horizon,
dirty February in the streets.
Rush to the florist, buy white lilacs,
timid violets, jonquils, anything
for pity of such guarded eyes
sabotaged by a smile
that ran away to join the circus
and now consorts with clowns, ignoring
the steel-eyed tightrope walkers.
Nobody walks on air
but fools and lovers.

THE PEARL FISHERS—BIZET

Caruso is singing
"Je crois entendre"
my opera-loving father's
favorite aria. What
in such wistful piece
charmed the feisty
man I remember,
a pilot in two wars
who still got in street fights
at fifty? He gave me his features
and now he has disappeared
into the green, green silence
of the pearl fishers' ocean—
treacherous as their quest.

Caruso's dead voice singing
of Nadir's lost, forbidden love
becomes my regret for all
unasked questions, my longing
for what is gone, gone forever
in a green, green depth
no pearl fisher can reach.

SKETCHBOOK

Paint me aware
of the rip
in my sister's thigh,
the crack in the pavement
growing a daisy,
the masks in people's lives,
paint me the green
of summer, in transparent
patches of memory,
paint me the heat
of early morning in July,
hide me
in your starry nights,
remember
remember me in the soft
rains of September,
paint me alive
in the snows to come.

THE GOLDEN TOUCH

Did Midas
watching the people
scramble for his meal
feel the desolate hunger
of the too-gifted,
whose only lot is giving,

as he cradled his cold
golden daughter
did he notice the swift
glance of the bazaar merchant
guessing what the child
could bring in ingots?

TRANSGRESSIONS

The summer I turned eight, at the lake house, I jumped down from our high garden wall on to the gravel of the shore and joined the gypsy children playing there. A golden, unfettered afternoon, though I almost sprained an ankle—and got lice. I've broken many rules since then, without paying the price, but that leap to a forbidden world brought swift and lively retribution. Days later, at the Grand Hotel up in the mountains, the crawling wages of my sin revealed themselves. Oh, the horror. Quickly quarantined in our room's bathroom, threatened to be sent back to the lake in disgrace, I itched, scratched and sobbed in vain con-trition, as I sat on the toilet, till Mother took pity on her lousy child and found a solution in purgatory. She put out a voice that I had sprained an ankle, ordered hot vinegar "for packs." For a whole day she doused my head with it, again and again, then shampooed, shampooed and fine-tooth combed till no evidence of my offense escaped alive. So long ago, but I still remember those intoxicating, burning, winey fumes, the endless fine-tooth combing for nits, the tingling of my purged scalp, the final, ambivalent feeling of loss and relief when, my trespass remedied, no longer an untouchable, I emerged glossy, deloused but unrepentant, the memory of forbidden, magic hours mingled forever with vinegar effluvia from my hair.

PANTA RHEI ?

"Everything flows"
−Heraclitus

We cannot step twice
in Heraclitus' water
and Leonardo's river
ever flows : *acqua passata*
over the dam, useless
as yesterday's newspaper,
the train we didn't board
and now pulls away.
The river cannot stop
seeking the sea.
Down in its depth
stones hold on.

> *«Ay, que trabajo*
> *me questa quererte como te quiero»*
>
> –Garcia Lorca

AY, QUE TRABAJO ME CUESTA

I peel your words, layer by layer
seeking a core of sweetness
I know is not there
and yet a part of me doesn't even care
to comfort my hands
white-knuckled, clutching your absence.

I dissect an inflection, put it under
the microscope, holding my breath
and then my eyes un-focus,
stray to the dancing leaves
outside the window, the children
 in the courtyard: pain
becomes an unfinished chore.

Poets make rather
poor worshipers: irreverent,
too easily side-tracked.
I play games with my grief
till I forget where I left it.
It takes days
to find its way home.

I bathe in your voice
looking for the hidden currents
like icy pathways in a Nordic lake.

But how I hate
the chill against my skin.

No, I don't begrudge
what it costs me to love you,
but, ay, it's uphill
work...

360

Once, in a winter storm, my car
skidded, churned me around
in a vortex of trees and snowy banks
fragmented to a mad kaleidoscope
then spewed me out the way
I meant to go. A perfect three-sixty.

Last week an overloaded boat capsized
between Malta and Lampedusa
in a serene blue night, three hundred
and sixty migrants drowned. Three
sixty. I see that number etched
in a cosmic chaos of unfair fates,
I see their smooth African skin,
blind eyes submerged asleep
in lost, different dreams, I feel
the pity of the our sea's accepting
them, mute flotsam in the path
of white cruise ships. I go
on those cruises, drive fast cars
too fast in the snow, get three-sixtied
unscathed. Surely, an abacus somewhere
is tallying my debts. Or is this weight
of a life undeserved the price to pay?

CHERRYDALE FLEA MARKET

The day doesn't seem to know
it's April, grey rain
chills the overpass
on the highway:
a cement catacomb.
We rummage
among other people's detritus
with numb fingers, looking
for hidden treasures
or just to wonder
at recycled
abandoned lives
for sale.

> *"Zénon! Cruel Zénon! Zénon d'Élee!"*
> *Le Cimetière Marin*
> Paul Valéry

THE BEGINNING

They sure can humble our ego
those Presocratics, shame a mind
weaned on lazy Wikipedia pap
as they wade, no compass,
into the uncharted possibilities
of the beginning. They leave us
flat-footed and amazed
at the wonder of Heraclitus' fire, of
Anaximander's germinal Infinite. And
Zeno, indeed so cruel
Zeno of Elea, forever pierces us
with his static arrow's endless flight
as we plod along with the turtle,
fossilized, full of unearned knowledge,
bound for destruction, yearning vainly
for a *tabula rasa* to test us, for a
glimpse of that primordial dawn.

BALLAD OF OTHER TIMES

If we had lived
in other times
I would have been your woman.
I would have gone with you
the day we met
along white roads,
dusty with summer,
behind your tinker's cart
from town to town.
On the feast days
of patron saints we would have laughed at
the dancing bear, watched mountebanks
perform, bargained for beads hawked by a
man who had been to the Holy Land with
Richard. Nights, we would have made
love in a haystack under a firefly sky,
distant dogs baying at the moon.

I would have borne you children,
nut-brown boys
with sky blue eyes
who never went to school
or wore shoes.
At the age that we are now
we would have been
old, or dead, a brief story played out.

Instead we are in our best
years: my picture makes
the society page, I collect black opals,
spend summers in Spain
and people seek your skills,
praise follows in your wake.
We might meet
at country clubs,
discuss the human condition,
exchange thieving stray glances
at parties.
When night comes, we retreat
to lie in the beds we have made.
To touch
is guilt.
And yet I was your woman
long time ago.

SHORTCUTS

If Dante had gone to Lugano
that Thursday, Holy Week in 1300,
instead of tangling with the *selva oscura,*
he could have saved himself a fearsome trip
down through the gates of Hell, then up
the scabrous, painful climb of Purgatory,
simply by boarding the Number 2 bus.
It takes you—a scenic ride—to *Paradiso.*

It would have been so easy.

But then, what of the damned,
naked, lost in the abyss, no hope of sky,
their tales in their mouths as they lined
his path begging for a connection,
a fleeting acknowledgement of *them,*
their human essence, not the sin.
So many, so many, forgotten, seeking
to exist again just even
for an instant in the weary
traveler's glance, in his listening ear.

No, it would have been no place
for shortcuts. How could Dante,
in his bitter compassion, choose
the easy way, add to Hell's terrors
the gnawing cruelty of indifference?

TOUCH

You have been dead many years
but suddenly last night—a quiet
rain—my hand again felt your skin,
that just-discovered, just-explored
male skin, so unexpectedly
smooth, so like mine,
a vulnerable twinning,
and love again flowed back, dumb
and blind in that quiet rain,
all senses distilled to a touch.

Yes, I still hold on
to our story, but my ears
have lost your voice
and eyes now need
a photograph to see you.
Even that inept, love-shy
girl who so loved you
is gone. But last night
a touch joined us again.

WALKING IN MILAN

All it takes is wisteria
freshly violet on white stucco walls,
a snowy drift
of poplar pollen in a doorway
to resurrect lost Aprils,
a child going to school
along this street. Fugitive houses
emerge in a transparency of water,
a bombed-out sweet shop
lures with forbidden
kaleidoscopes of candies,
blissful licorice sticks
tell-tale black on the tongue.
By the boarded-up barracks
homeless ghosts of *barboni*
shrouded in the rags
of their eternal winter
again cue up for the soup
soldiers doled out at noon
to outstretched tin pails,
to blighted lives I watched
and couldn't understand.

The past exiles me. I stand
invisible on this familiar street
and watch usurpers go by,
invading hordes who now own
my city. But they will never own
my submerged Atlantis,
its barren barracks, that square

where olive-clad soldiers
long dead in a forgotten war
once more ladle out hope
to derelict ghosts. I taste
a bittersweet licorice on my tongue
and clusters of amethyst return
on a wisteria that will be
blooming forever, just for me.

SELECTIONS FROM

The Snow on Lake Como

GRAFFITI AT THE COMO RAILROAD STATION

I

The rain that whips dormant oleanders
along the lake shore—in the garden
of the Hotel du Lac vanquished camellias
press their inmate pallor to the fence—
last night covered the peaks with April snow.
On water grey as November
a steamer arches from the pier,
shudders, moans goodbye. Blurred seasons
brings disoriented longings,
years lose their scaffold.
Other departures surface.

Autumn a day like this. My father and I
walk from the steamer landing to the train.
He is already in uniform, blue-grey. Rain spatters
my new school shoes. Between us, subdued on
a slack leash, the bristle-coated German hound
who went to war with him. That dog could
smile. Dead leaves
from the horse-chestnut tree rust
on the sidewalk, pods spiked like mines.
The trees today are heavy in bloom, milestone
of a journey I've yet to understand.
It rained for days
and all my shoes are wet.

II

The waiting room at the station opens
like a time capsule: hardwood benches
built to begrudge support for troubled hopes
of emigrants, for evening surges of evacuees
fleeing the night air-raids. Askew in a corner
a broken 1940's scale, pointer fixed on 30 kilos
—the weight of the child I was then. On the wall,
teen-age obscurity scrawled in magic marker:
Gianna and Lella are seeking "*tosti*" boys,
someone who cannot spell promises
undefined violence to "our enemies"

"I'm tall, handsome, blond, with green eyes'
I like big fruit"—for an instant, naïve maturity
conjures apples, pears, slender boughs bent under
a ripened weight— "Boys with bulging jeans, call
Fabio." A phone number. Third digit smudged—
flash of sanity, pentimento or simply a bored
child licking the wall ("Don't do that, Sandro")
when the train was late?

It could be a joke. Will the math professor,
the old-maid neighbor receive an obscene call
or is this the boy no one desired? Spread-eagled
on this wall as on a dirty sheet, does a dream
persona waits to be impaled, the victim luring
his tormenters to perdition? Why do I know
this is a message on a prison wall,
the bottle on the wave? We are all
nailed to some wall, Fabio.

III

The night refugees in the child's eyes
have long since tumbled into death, my father
first to the pit, his hair still bright. Where,
which are the victims now, Fabio? Are green-eyed
blonds immune? Even Sappho's apple
must fall to winter winds. We do not choose
our seasons. But on rainy springs
horse-chestnut trees still push
their pink-veined flowers upward, small mouths
open wide to the sky, undefeated, greedy as birds.

NOSTALGIA LATINA

Bring me words that fill the mouth like apricots,
stone-smooth, fruited with vowels,
words with earth clinging to their roots,
bring me sure-footed words, with the serene
heft of a mossy goddess in the sun
scorning her broken arms, the quiver full of rain
and I won't heed these Saxon sounds,
thorny stars, precise violets.
Bring me words like water in the sun.

EVENING OF THE FIESTA

Concertina
in the sky, columnar
wish to be dead, a swaying
clarity pierced by grief
of dim horizons, unknown birds.
The sea folds its tents,
gives nothing away. Naked
street lights bloom across the plaza,
take on the night.
Summer dies in the skeletons
of butterflies, the incurable
presence of nothing, unanswerable
as the dead bulls, unneeded love.....

CABO DE LAS HUERTAS

An afternoon cantilevered over blue,
August in Spain. A drowsy sea
mumbles content against the reef.

A day like a revisited childhood.

Of the orchards
that gave the place its name
nothing is left
but a few ruined walls
bleached white by salt—twisted trunks
evoke ghosts of apricots. A marine
cemetery. Only the fig trees
have survived
by running away, becoming wild.
High above, the lighthouse squints,
crumbly stucco
whitewashed to blinding light.

Siesta silence. Under the promontory
an off-duty busboy
caresses his ballooning
faceless girlfriend. She sways
to some inner music, at her feet
seaweeds die in the sun
like paper chains.

By the lighthouse wall
the fat sergeant of the Guardia Civil—
rivulets of sweat streaming from the shiny

carapace of his hat through day-old stubble—
has planted a meager rose bush
that tries to bloom. The black
roses of Paestum lived in kinder times.
We have outgrown the curse of simpler
gods, our Furies scream by in a red Ferrari

SEPTEMBER MORNING AT THE LIDO

One thinks of course of Thomas Mann
and the boy, not so much the dated
one of the book (that sailor suit,
the poor teeth) but rather the epicene
ephebus of the movie as he stood here
scuffing the sand, glancing back
at ruined middle age with calm
unfeeling eyes, in a September morning
such as this, where sand, water and sky
become one clarity, as if the sinking city,
washed by the sea, were re-emerging here
in pale primordial light, a new
third day, but scaled down, human.

VENICE UNDER THE SNOW

A girl in a red coat crosses the square,
her footprints linger in the snow.
This is a place of shifting truths: streets ebb
with the tide, stone facades ripple, slide in
the canals. Lions have wings
and can read.

Wild ducks return
to hide among the reeds
at Torcello. A funeral
of gondolas glide by.
And snow descends, fills the outstretched hand
of a grey saint pleading from his niche.
In the folds of his cowl a pigeon
shivers and sleeps.

AIRPORT HIGHWAY, NEW ORLEANS

The sign by the Lutheran church ramp
says "Atonement this exit" but so easy
a slide surely only leads to sin. Indulgences,
maybe—they've been sold before. Why not a drive-in?
But atonement is winterkill, is Henry at Canossa.
bare feet in the snow, his penitent's sackcloth
ripped by the hunger of a wolf-wind howling
deep in the Apennines. Only the evergreen,
like hate, could have endured. Didn't the old man
biding his time by the fire in the great hall
know that no one forgives
being forgiven? Did Mathilda
fur cloak brushing silently on stone steps,
descend at night in the ice of the courtyard
to bring the imperial beggar food, to offer
her lamp-lit face for warmth?
Back on his throne, could he
forgive her charity? There is
no exit. Both women and men today dance
naked on the bars in Bourbon street.

THINGS I LEARNED IN SURGERY

Veins are really blue. Arteries,
though are white, till you cut them.

Adhesions over the liver
are called violin strings.
They make no music.

Sterility is like pregnancy: things
are either sterile or not. But one
can be sterile and pregnant.

In local anesthesia you never say "Whoops".
Instead you say, "There now."

The heart hides in a sac
and squirms.

When you remove a clamp from the carotid
and blood squirts five feet up in the air
and hits the overhead lamp, the correct
clinical assessment is "Oh, shit."

The fissure of Roland
is in the brain, not at Roncevaux.

Nobody knows the real function of the spleen.

When someone says "Will you be here tomorrow?"
it often means "Will I be here tomorrow?"

MOONLIGHT

Diana Trivia
sits at the crossroad
and gives no sign,

no wonder
the dark face of the moon
consorts with thieves.

The wolf
was given
a burning stone for bread.

Homemade
deep in his throat,
deceit flames, lights

the forest
with golden eyes
portholes of hell.

Knives of ice
glisten. Astarte
travels the winter night.

THE AMBUSH

I didn't know the ambush
would come in a dream: a country road
twisting away between two cliffs—I rounded
a boulder and there it was: your loss,
like an unburied child
reproaching my easy breath.
I had thought our parting
a smooth divergence of water. Those cliffs so
deviously green knew better. The tangle of
life lines surfaced, hidden nets dragged the
stream, churned up dead days. I recognized
moments, belly up on the bank, the eyes
already glazing: the night we wrapped
the electric blanket around the cherry tree to
keep it warm, the flowers you forgot
you had sent me. I closed my shoulders
against their silence, went on. Indifference
already grew around the dog that ran away.

LOOKING BACK

You know the danger
of looking back: Orpheus, or the other one
turned into salt because of a last glimpse
at a red tile roof, a branch
of the fig tree planted in the courtyard
when she was a bride. The fruit
so carefully picked, the newly spun
flax on the loom: what does a god care
about such things? Go on, they say
forget about the unwanted dog
that tags along just out of reach, hoping
you'll change your mind. Look
forward, don't regret
the dark cool oil waiting for the lamp.

DRIVING TO AN UNKNOWN PLACE
FOR THE WEEKEND

I think of adventurers, the secret ones
who go out for cigars and disappear
(at our summer place
the baker had done just that
in 1910—old men
sunning themselves on lakeside benches
still spoke of it.) We call them
runaways. But who knows
what compass guides the heart?
Traces of snow
in the gullies, marsh-green
fields : expectant desolation
of earth in February. All familiar
enough. So why this feeling
of a discovery impending, a sign pointing
to a secret way?
As to the baker
word came back that he was baking bread
in Buenos Aires. The water there
was like ours, just right for the yeast.

THE SQUARE AT VIGEVANO

For E.V. d M.

Swan Lake

I lived for years in a Russian winter
fairytale, swans gliding on a stage and
the snow falling on St. Petersburg
because of you. I was the black
ugly duckling, twice as rare, twice
as far to go. You were the first
lake, mirror of possibility, magician
conjuring out of snow and secret dark
a girl-swan's slowly unfurling wings.
Each winter the spell returns. I know
you exist somewhere in a lost country
where snow swirls under a glass dome.
Odette-Odile, the swans are
your elusive emissaries, beckoning,
gliding out of reach.

November 2nd

"He's not here," your Venetian houseman said
the last time I called. I didn't know
you were dying in a clinic, in Rome. But today
on this beach swept clean of every hope of summer
I know how here, really, the dead are—they walk
in the void at my shoulder. If I turn around
I surprise only air, nothing moves,
but the dead are here. My father
walks out of the home woods
with his shot gun, becomes you
standing at the edge of the rice fields,
in other Novembers, unloading the shells,
while the dogs run ahead, cross down to this sand
nose to the wind, sniffing
the snows soon to come.

Truffles

The gourmet market has for sale
white truffles: two runty ones
plain as dirt, the color of dried clay,
a trace, barel, of lost violets,
of woodbine. Half-buried in raw rice
in the cheese case, they stab with recognition:
an autumn dormant in their spores
breaks out. No, Proust was wrong. The past
is a child the gypsies took away:
it grows up by itself, will disown us
when we meet. The truffles in the rice
just squat exuding memories, ignore me.

I know their woods, when dead leaves turn
silent under rain and early fog disembodies
the trees. A chestnut falls, opens its wound.
Winter is near, the earth goes to earth.
The time we bought truffles
at Alba under the arcades,

fog erased the road on the way home,
became a river of ghosts. "If we see Charon"
you said, "hide." The truffles filled
the car with sweet decay.

Corners

The building on the corner where you used
to wait for me has been torn down,
the pastry shop is gone,
but ghost lights hover on the pavement, gleam
on the hood of your car
and I again come hurrying up the street
breathless, as if I had run all my young years
toward that moment. You were always there.

A half-torn poster on a kiosk. The circus we
knew is back in town. Are we the needle
gyrating on the compass? I have traveled so
far and never moved. Around the corner
your absence waits. Invisible,
a wrecker's ball dismantles days like bricks.

The Square at Vigevano

Now that you are dead, your image has become
a silent film clip frozen on the screen,
unchangeable. I can no longer dream
different endings to our story, some

last reprieve. This evening in the square
fog descends, licks the cobblestones,
the arcades recede, float toward the unknown
that walls you away from anything we shared.

I didn't need to see you again, I wanted
only the possibility. I am haunted
by this nothing flung between you and me
that makes the past a broken bridge, reality
a no man's land for memory. You were
the exile's lost country, unreachable but there.

ADVENT

It's cold. I watch people in the street
faces averted, shoulders bent
in penitence. December
precipitates at the bottom of the year,
January will be a stretch in solitary.
Christmas returns. And again I am
going from castle to castle
in search of you. The ground
is stone under my feet,
I am breathing glass.

I've piled pyramids
of apples, burst the fragrance
of tangerines. Somebody
brings holly and balsam for the door.
The forest enters my house.

Evergreens burn in the wind,
the wolf is sent to the slaughter.

Under the fur, under the glitter
hunger rages, howls in the night.
I can't reach you
and the stars are nailheads.

Snows rim the footprints
of passers-by, the street loses its
name. Out in the garden
ice traps goldfish in the pond.

KALEVALA

Beyond the evergreens
at the edge where things
let go, subside into the silence
of earth deep in winter

the circular river girds the snow.
Here in a stillness
as if the dead where listening the
black swan comes, glides his slow

patterns on the dark waters
perfectly alone. No one
to hear his song: the fool is still away
and will fail, as he must. Solitude

is no country for fools. One trades
in harsh coin here: empty mirrors
drowning uncautious images,
whispering doubts, days

like mouths to feed. The swan
only knows a stillness of dark waters,
a snowy silence. And his song, to mask the
humming of the arrow, when it comes.

THE HORN OF ROLAND

Durandal, sword,
arm of my arm, you survive all frays
while I lie spent, the tapestry of my days
rent by a traitor's word,

see, the radiance
abates, birds fly home to their nests
as they have gone to eternal peace, best
flowers of France

asleep at noon
with staring eyes, wind in the wild thyme
calling the bees, blood in their mouth like wine
drawn too soon,

is their death my
last sin: should I have sooner let the horn
reverberate our need, cry our forlorn
plea to the sky,

was the pursuit
too late for rescue, or has pride such deep
roots in my soul that only death should reap
its barren fruit?

No, the meeting
was fated long ago. I was a green
boy dreaming of glory and the Saracen
blade was here waiting,

a planted seed
brings forth the form it is meant to take,
cannot change its inborn nature, make
oak out of reed,

I die for the glory
of an old man who listen to betrayers and
will remember in his evening prayers for
a while. The story

will be told by the fire
how we died young, Hector in his prime
forever mourned. Death before its time
lights the pyre,

gives song to a lay
that miniates the carnage in the gorse,
the stench, the plunging of a maddened horse
riderless in the fray...

I want my life!
I want to feel a girl cling, cleave under me,
drift in the slumber of satiety,
a honeyed strife

in newly stacked hay,
hay in our hair, a sky of fireflies,
a far dog challenging the moon, its cries
echoing away...

It grows cold, I hear
a hunting horn. Is it winter? Unhood
the peregrine. Yes, the hunting will be good
this time of year...

GALATEA

Your hand were borrowed from the
Delphi Charioteer: there is metal
in their caress that scrapes my cheekbones,
traces the subterranean path of the blood
along the skin, the blooming
of breasts from stone
while I kneel
and listen to myself
being born in the pleasure
of your distant eyes.
And you don't know
the agony of statues
wrenched into life by kisses
in sunlit parks. Buy them
sunglasses, so they can hide.
What will they do
naked in the street?

EURYDICE

There is no color in this place, only a weightless
grey where land merges into sky—maybe this is
the sky, and shadows I see are passing clouds
in human shape. I am a shadow myself— my
hands over my face don't hide me. In that other
place there bloomed a field of hyacinths. When I
fell their blue closed over me as if I'd fallen
into sky. The pain snaking through, a scream
dying away in the valley, was lost in that cool
charity. Blue faded to grey. Later, when he
appeared, his eyes hyacinthine flames in the mist
and said, "Come," I didn't ask him where,
but went with him because of those flowers
in his eyes. He knew, he could hold the smoke
that was my hand. And I held on to him
as we walked, sunless shadows in that grey.
Under his touch I could feel my blood
resurfacing to sing in the mute skin, my hand
a waking bird in his. We walked—stones
grew sharp under my feet, the pain resurged.
When he suddenly said, "We must go back,"
I felt glad. Now I could guide him. He turned to glance
back at a shadow beyond us on the path. I wanted him
to look only at me. "**Come**," I said. A smile
rippled his eyes, like wind across blue hyacinths.

CYGNET

When winter came
and the sky changed to lead
the pond began to freeze
at the rim; his life
shrank into ever-narrowing
circle, till one night
the ice trap snapped. The farmer
found him in the morning,
brought him in.
You know the disasters
before he found an open window
and escaped.

Early April
the farmer's wife
saw a flash of snow
on the pond: great
outspread wings
whiter than her linen,
an arrogant neck. Staring
from the small head
the eyes of that filthy
half-crazed beast
who had upset her churn,
smashed her crockery. That night
as she braided her graying hair
she asked her husband to shoot it.

THE PRODIGAL SON

The fatted calf deserved better
than this papa's boy
whimpering repentance at the gate.
I feel for the old man: children
are fissures in the heart. But he, the son,
resting the day after in the courtyard,
telling his tale to the servant girl,
how could he bear to see compassion
for his maimed wings in her earthbound eyes?
He gives us wayward travelers a bad name.
Let the heavens rejoice for the lost sheep
rescued from brambles while obedient ones
huddle unprotected in the cold.
Give the meek their inheritance. I'll take
Lucifer's side.

TAPESTRY

"Verrà la morte e avrà I tuoi occhi"
–C. Pavese

After the feast
Death will come from the hills
walking the rim of night, releasing dream
like heat waves from the pavement. Below
the city sleeps along the river.
Down from the woods
shadows gather under bridges,
slip silently in the water. Unmoored,
the past flows by.
You wear the eyes
of a Condottiere
ugly-mouthed on your bronze horse,
I wear the long summer
you came north with your troops
and laid siege to my city. Flowers
bloom in the moat
across my chest, sway in the current.

Time clots like blood in the night heat,
my bones will be a necklace for a chieftain.
I remember the rain on our surrender.

Death will come with your eyes.
your trick of a sudden smile
meaning nothing,
a forgotten land mine
maiming children at a picnic.

And Death will have my eyes
that watched you ride on your bronze horse
over the bridge, into the rain.

THE SNOW ON LAKE COMO

I

Back to the house after the funeral
we huddled by the black iron stove hastily
lit to chase the shut-up chill of unused
rooms and waited for the cars. A maid
passed the black comfort of coffee.
Few mourners: my father's people,
come to bury his widow,
some of the villagers. Cousins
I remembered as children of summers long
past, running into this room
with fishing poles—small faces
barely sketched in, high-pitched voices—
now had begun to wear
their dead parents' features.
From across the lake,
my mother's shore, had come unknown old
ladies, relicts of her youth. From fringed
dark furs, each waxwork face
emerged naked as a condor's head
beaky, the skin too close
to the skin.

The usual conversation
about the flowers, the blessing
of a long life, and going so quickly. Such
a sunny day for February.
But the walk up to the mountain cemetery,
our grey chapel with its wall

of neatly waiting pigeon-holes, the same names
knelling on each slab—only the dates
told them apart—those glass-enclosed
photographs where people look
truly dead, distorted
as on the back of a spoon,
had brought *memento mori*. Even the coffee
couldn't help. "That young priest!"—
my sister plucked an easy
scapegoat out of the air—
"One hour in an unheated church! We'll have
an epidemic on our conscience."
The tenant farmer's daughter, who soloed
in the choir, promised come next Sunday
he'll get a piece of her mind.

Childhood paints memories
on unsized canvas. Revisited,
a house shrinks like an old woman's bones,
disorients with the subtle treason
of inanimate things. Only the mountains
un-comprehended before, now revealed their
glaciers, impervious, opaque as dead men's
mirrors. One summer two climbers became
stuck on the north face, had to be rescued.
From our garden wall, binoculars propped
against a fork on the wisteria,
we saw them dangle in a web of ropes
like inept spiders. The grown-ups watched
the rescue all day.

II

We were to spend the night across the lake
with a maternal cousin—drive down to Lecco
then up the other shore. Up-lake, the road—
a ledge between mountain and water—
cuts deep into the rock: shafts of sunlight
stab though arched fissures where the lake
flashes blue. At Lecco the mountains
let go, the lake slips swift
under the bridge, emerges as a river
and winds away, flat in the flat plain
toward the Po, the ultimate
lure of the sea.

We stopped for tea. The lakefront
café was a greenhouse
of promised spring: mimosas,
violets in white vases, even anemones
on the tea cups. The flowers on the bier
had been carnations, stiff,
aggressively pink. "They'll survive
anything" the florist in Milan had said
when I explained the burial at the lake,
"while this…" He shook his head at a mimosa,
yellow duckling, cheering up a corner.

Outside the café, the promenade
empty, windswept. By the deserted
embarcadero, rowboats pulled up
on the broad steps, swaddled in canvas,
sleeping pharaohs, chrysalides. On the terrace

wind prodded the coils
on an abandoned scarf,
blue snake, too cold
To slither away.

III

Bellagio. Tip of the peninsula,
my mother's childhood place. Soft-hued
eighteen century villas, moored
in botanical parks: camphor, sandalwood
Tibetan pine, cork. A living
chinoiserie. At the lake's edge, homier
willows drowning uncautious
branches in the still water — a warning
to children sneaking a forbidden swim.

My mother's father had sea-blue eyes
and a greenhouse with a mimosa plant
that would recoil when touched. *Sensitiva*. He
had studied gardening in Germany
as a young man. His graduation picture shows
him blond, high-button coat, one elbow on a
Corinthian column
and those clear eyes.

IV

The cousin's husband, a botanist. pointed out
his own trees: monkey puzzle,
banana wrapped in straw,
exiled Zulus stranded in a Nordic winter.
Sheltered in a hollow
a rare find, an Asiatic palm tree
exotic infant born—he used the word—
the summer day when men stepped on the moon.
We peered in the descending dusk, admired
like people shown through a softly opened door,
their host's sleeping children.

In the morning, it snowed. Smudged by
white fingers lake and peninsula
blurred to mist, disappeared. In the
garden the snow shaped the empty
flower beds into soft rectangles,
fresh graves.

SELECTIONS FROM

Exile at Sarzana

"LIKE SNOW ON A WINDLESS ALP"

As I leave the Italian Store
—a ciabatta , fresh mozzarella—
it begins to snow. Large
weightless flakes drift down
from an infinite sky in a white silence
that mutes the traffic on Lee Highway, dims
the bright neon of the pawnbroker's shop.
I stand there in the cold, errands
forgotten as a line by Dante
blooms up from far recesses
of high-school memory:"*Come di neve
in alpe senza vento."* For a moment
time is erased. That windless snow
now descends quietly on us both,
the same flakes melting on our skin
as we pause to look up at a gray nothing
that unites us, him in a bitter winter
at Ravenna, surviving on the salty
bread of exile, and me exiled here
among parked cars, clutching
this stylish food that he too ate,
bridged through the centuries between us
by the circular mystery of existence.

VOLTERRA

The fields mount toward the rock
in yellow-green swells—a tide
of wheat stubble, olive leaves
rushes up to menace walls that flee
heavenwards. You think of Titans
and assaults in the sky.
Or, maybe, Saint Augustine.

A city like a well, the same
elemental sufficiency: stone,
hidden water. Even the pool
at the hotel seems a cistern,
hoarded, ready for a siege. A black
scissor-tailed swallow
sweeps down to drink, soars,
sweeps across the pool again,
becomes a messenger, the winged
arrow over the wall that signals
take heart, help is on the way.
But down below in the plain
an army of sunflowers
turns ruffled heads away.
They will not come.

In the kiln of the sun
rooftops bleach to the bones
of long-dead summers—you hear
the sand flow in the hourglass.
But time is not an adversary,
here. A flowerpot shard crumbles

under your sandal, terracotta dust
reshapes itself into a primal form:
an earlier sun beats down, July
has yet no name and an Etruscan girl
dips water from a jar under the black
shade of a plum tree. She smiles
the smile of those who know
and won't tell.

What did they know, these Etruscans
so hooked on Hades
they scrambled to get there
any which way, foot, chariot,
boat. Why this nostalgia
for the deep cool earth,
its mossy silence?
You watch them lounge
on their sarcophagi
as if on stony sofas,
serene, fulfilled,
perusing entrails
like a daily horoscope.
But one looks straight
at you, eyes of a satyr,
and thin lips bow upwards.

At sunset, in the piazza
old men gather, sit on stone
benches by the duomo: they've always
been here, like the stones,

the swallows, this purple
vespertine sky. But sand
glides in the hourglass
and you are the sand. Down
below, the horizon exiles the sun.

STREET MUSICIANS, LUCCA

The Peruvian boys dance
in a circle, a slight
syncopation
in their step
a vestige
of ritual rhythms
undulated
as the sweet
reedy music
thin as Andean
air pierces
the Tuscan evening
with alien longings
of migratory birds
stranded across oceans
across seasons
to this street
in the heat
of Lucca in July.

MESON DEL COSO

Alicante

Fernando
bailaor flamenco,
eyes
of a woman betrayed,
disdain of centuries
in the mouth,
make-up stains
on the frills of his shirt.
A lean, hungry boy,
maricon,
who dreams of Hollywood
while a turista
at the back table
dreams of Spanish dancers.
Murky longings
twang from a guitar.
Ole', we cry
as we eat *caracoles,*
spear tired olives
with banderillas.
"*Quando un hombre
me penetra*" Fernando whispers
"*yo siento como una mujer.*"
Tomorrow
the sun will rise,
tonight we live
in borrowed skin.
So cry me a river
of sangria,
let the guitar's

pulse fill the blood.
The meson's owner
is named Jesus.
Maybe
we will be saved.

END OF DAY

Attilio Simonetti
(Barbizon School, ca. 1890)

February. The month of dirty snow
and grey souls. Evening. Slow
homeward trudge along a country road
rutted by carts—slush seeping in,
shackling exhausted feet.
Silhouettes of houses at the horizon
hold no promise of warmth. Black
gibbet trees blur the edge of dusk.

But high above
a vampire sunset glows
with winter fire, drains
all life from the land,
inflames the puddles
with fragments of some high Eldorado,
a Civitas Dei no one can reach
but it's there. Ask your grief
to be wise. The day is ending—
see, dark rest will come.

FISHTAIL LODGE, POKHARA
(Nepal)

Someone out on the lake
is playing "Fur Elise"
on a flute. Can music
make landscapes alien
to themselves, exile
that tree by the raft landing
like the Tibetan refugees
hawking beads in its shade,
their need our daily gantlet?
We cross on the lodge raft
at will, an easy glide
between two worlds—no
question of salvation
here: limpid waters,
no Charon, a flute.

Why then the unbidden
asp in the reeds:
how shall we answer
for the dispossessed
and save ourselves?
As to the armless boy
watching us click
our cameras (who dressed him
in that striped shirt,
who feeds him?) his silence
weighs like a judgement.
Out on the lake
you can hear his ghost hands
playing that flute. No,
we will not save ourselves.

SKY BURIAL

Tibet

The *Assumption of the Virgin*
painted by Titian in the Frari church
holds no more mystery than this
sublimation by vulture, this ultimate
recycling: disappear, consumed
by creatures born of this hypnotic
sky--bluer than any heaven
you could hope for--flesh
lacerated, bones crushed to a meal
to feed the hungry. Surely
an act of mercy recorded, a last chance
to do some good. And surely
better than putrefaction, slow
decay to a few trace minerals
for nourishing wild flowers
that couldn't grow here anyway.
Fire? It would release toxic
thoughts, pollute the crystal air.
No, far better this renewed
tie to Prometheus. Imagine him
unbound, redeemed, ascending
among fierce-beaked, taloned
dark-winged angels.

THE CASTLE
To K., the Land Surveyor

I

Perhaps your strength was innocence,
the fool's charmed armor. Maybe
it was submerged remembrance of
a previous time, when clearer eyes
could read the Runic pitting
on ice-cracked boulders, divine
a future cast like molten lead
by tangled winter branches
on moonlit snow. And perhaps
when you stopped for a moment
on the bridge and looked up,
it was just faith—the belief
in a promise given long ago
and reneged on along the way:
there is a meaning to the voyage—
hope cannot be a sin to be expiated.

II

It is always deepest winter,
always evening, when we reach
that unnamed village blanketed
in snow. Huddled, silent houses,
where few windows glow secret
like banked embers. We sense
the castle in the void above,
in the doorless grey fog that mutes
our steps, dissolves in mist
the lifeline of the traveled road
at our back. It's a bitter

cold night, and we come from nothing.
Did Franz echo here winters in Prague,
a castle that cuts into thin air,
severs the bond between earth and sky?
Is this the longing that impelled you—
and us—to this place? Are we your kin,
exiles in our own skin, exiles
from a country we don't know?

III

Sunset flames leaded windows
makes the village houses blind.
The Castle holds impervious. No
message comes, no password. There's
no thaw here, no hope of spring,
the sky is a glass bell
where voices grow mute and die.
Eyes look away. We are
danger, we who won't give up.

VI

We won't give up. Limpid-eyed
as born liars, sharp-eared, full
of tricks, we'll go to earth
in a furrow, become fertile seed
under the snow. Our legs
will intertwine, sink roots
in the dark, secret soil. And there
we'll wait with you. Our stubborn
breaths will mingle, streak the winter air
like a path to the sky, a newborn star.

CASTLES IN AIR

The trick
was in teaching
the stones
to float,
in devising
an invisible mortar
that bound and freed,
like love. The turrets
were easy: they shot up
like rockets
at the four corners
and held.

Yet the dreams
were too heavy.

THE INMATES

Venus in Furs
is in a cage
at the zoo

and we dandle
our aberrations
upon our knees—

unwanted children
cared for
but not loved.

The wall
holding us in
is the fear
in your eyes.

When night comes
we dance barefoot
on shards
of broken dreams.

PAVANE FOR A DEAD PRINCESS

(Ravel)

Don't read hope
in my hand,
it only holds
the gift of my emptiness
masked in the arabesque
of a court dance,
don't read a plea
in the fall of my sleeve,
it only hides
the tugging strings.
I asked no promise
when our eyes
met in the mirror
where I must exist.

But as you watch me leave
this golden room,
sense my warmth
under this shrouding
brocade, trace
my silent mouth
with a healing finger.
I have heard
that skies can be blue.

THE STARS OF THE BEAR

"Vaghe stelle dell'Orsa"
                    –Leopardi

I

November. A huntress moon stalks her prey
across the nitid sky—a small star
freezes, rabbit ensnared by headlight--
looking for a kill, clean and round
and perfect as herself. But the She-Bear
sleeps in another hemisphere tonight,
hibernates in the past as in her cave
of ice--and fears no arrows
nor unleashed remembrance.

II

I'm five, the night of my birthday,
barefoot in the garden and someone
says: "Look! Look at the bears!
Can you see them?" as I search the sky
for a great muzzle, a strong paw
hooking a salmon in the Milky Way
like the bear in my book, who likes
fish and blueberries. But I only
see stars, a thousand galactic fireflies
dancing above my head, a stellar vertigo
rotates in an abyss that sucks me in
so that I must crouch and grasp the grass
by my feet or I shall fall into the sky.
And then I see them, the bear and her cub,
the wondrous menagerie of the void
parade under the big top, starry fur
twinkling electric, heavy body

a-sway with the music of the sphere
around and around, till they merge
in a jumble of stars, disappear
as if it had been all a trick, worse,
a glimpse of Eden. For the first time
I taste exile.

III

And does it ever end, this sensing
that it should have been different,
the fruit not eaten, the right path
easier to recognize? The trees
bore no sign post and the she-wolf,
the lion and the lynx have become
fellow travelers. The *selva oscura*
has gone like the rain forest--soon
there'll be no trees in Madagascar
and Polaris no longer shows the way.
Constellations revolve in horoscopes
in a newspaper--inane promises
eclipsed by the headlines. Time
is a turbulent river sweeping
by, snaring the past in a net of stars,
present and lost like the Great Bear.

THE KING OF A RAINY COUNTRY

"Je suis comme le roi d'un pays pluvieux"
–Baudelaire

In my kingdom where rain
never-ending, quiet as a blade between two
ribs, slips in to quell the surging of a heart
still unruly, in this palace draped
with ennui like grey silk,
where tarnished mirrors yawn opaque,
stagnant ponds no animal drinks from,
the ladies of the court bare coral breasts
to the crown on my head with avid boredom,
glide into my bed—pearl rosary
smooth and untouched under my fingers,
cool flesh as unquencing
as the memory of water.

We embark for cold Cythaeras
that exile the heart, pretend
pastorals in the stables,
change gold to straw. Even
the sad eyes of the horses,
all-accepting, the warm
cloud of their breath can't warm me.

It's then, in the resigned
metronome of rain on the tin roof
that comes the echo of other
possibilities, a distant land
rife with storms
and violent sunsets,

burning azures that bleach the earth,
scour it bone-clean. Water there
becomes a lifeline on my hand.
And in that land a woman
with severe brow and quiet eyes,
whom I shall never know,
waits for me, and judges and forgives me.

FOG

If this morning, as I awoke to a white
invisibility and by a sudden witchcraft
it was Milan's fog out there, that winter
pressing against the window, a pale revenant,

if from that doorless nothing you came back
and a remembered need pierced sharp
and silent, an ambushing blade
sudden against the heart,

if the fog sponged the years away,
ephemeral chalk on a slate,
don't think, love, it's because
I still miss you—I've learned too many

ways to survive. No, perhaps I miss
what I was, that overserious
naive girl who thought to die for love
would have been a good thing. She went

with you in that spellbound winter
and the fog holds you in thrall. I can't
find the sign, the sorcerer's incantation
that will bring you both back or let me go.

VIA CERVA

Perhaps it was the silence of your house
obviously empty but serene, aloof
from the ephemeral fury of rush hour
clogging Via Cerva this evening—like
someone who has stepped ouside events

and managed to bypass change—or maybe
it was looking at your bedroom window
from the outside, the glass so clean,
so hard against this vulnerable sky,
briar rose blurred by poplar pollen

of a too-dry May—a month we never
made love in—but suddenly the old
sense of exile welled up, a silent
flood, unstemmed, uncheckable. It was
as when you stand in San Marco square

and the *acqua alta* seeps up from a drain
and stones and pigeons tremble in amphibious
abiguity. I still don't understand
this hold unfinished things
seem to possess—a barbed hook buried

under the skin, healed over, till a trick
of light reels you back, a window
ripples like an autumn pond disturbed by
an acorn, **smoke rises in** the air with
the smell of leaves burning—a crow,

long dead, caws in the horn of a car.
Maybe, there is no sense to this,
the long ribbon of years, and who dies
and who goes on.

For surely there is no earthly fairness
to my standing here, reasonably unscathed
and brooding about the meaning of love,
while people are killed in Sarajevo
as they cue for bread. No archduke
this time, only old women, lying
in their black dresses and their blood.

But perhaps, in spite of *panta rhei*
and Leonardo and his river, our fate
is simply recurrence. We can't escape
Gavrilo Princip and the carnage of this day
nor the return of blooms on the wisteria,

the snowy afterthought of pollen.
Nor your being still here, my own beloved
living dead, benign Dracula who comes
back when I least expect you, perennial
joker in the pack. It's right

that you should own me again, a girl
etched by time and different loves,
pausing to look at a briar-rose
May in your window while the evening
descends on Via Cerva and on us.

MARCH STORM

The storm that encased naked branches
into spun glass this morning--echoes
of Christmas in Imperial Vienna,
icicle chandeliers, doomed waltzes
at Mayerling with Rudolf and Maria-
has softened into flowers
of snow, a remembered
Majorcan spring: almond groves
in bloom and the new-born sea's
quiet breathing. I had forgotten
that day in March, the steep path
down to a beach where the seaweeds
still held winter's spent fury
in long green fingers. But now,
these icy flowers bring it back
and with it you, and the weight
of unmade choices. Suddenly,
the past turns as precarious
as tomorrow. Nothing remains.
Those white peacocks we watched
strut raucous on the terrace
at Formentor are ghosts, the flowered
branches retreat barren into winter
and no one knows what is to come.

THINKING OF YOU ON A MARCH MORNING

The day tries to hold on to winter,
but the forsythia is out, trumpets yellow
against the fence. From my window

I watch the breakfast of the birds
in the backyard. Sleet doesn't fool
them. They know what is coming. I drink

my tea and find no need to read
the leaves. I, too, know what's
coming. But like the day, I fear

to lose what's gone. I try to remember
your voice, but too many seasons
have changed guard. Sleet blurs

your face, strands you in a country
we never inhabited, as if you had
been shot at the border while

we tried to escape (some obsolete
cold war, a field still dirty
with March snow) and I had to leave

you there, bleeding through the years
while I went ahead, safe, into a new
country that would not, could not know us.

THREE CHINESE POEMS

Waiting

I'm kneeling on the river bank,
my reflection shimmers in the water.
But I am filled with sadness.
I don't hear your footsteps on the path
and your face
is not mirrored next to mine.
Maybe you'd like to come
but have doubts:
will it be enough,
this quiet house
in the woods by a river?
Or perhaps you fear
no one is waiting?

Nocturn

The pillow still holds the imprint of your head,
in the fireplace the flames have died down.
Out in the moonless winter night
cold stars glitter.

Leaving

I've worked so hard
to bring beauty in the house.
I've woven fragrant rushes for the rooms
and hung soft yellow lanterns by the door.
Now that you've come
and are resting on the moon-strewn bed,
I'm told I don't belong here
and I must leave.
I will go out of the gate one morning,
when frost rims the path with icy flowers.
All that I own
remains here.
On the road I will stop a cart,
ask to be taken far away.
As the cold fields waken
I will lay my head
on my empty hands,
closing my eyes
I'll try not to dream.

WINTERS

You said: "Remember that one day
you will forget me. It's true,
I know," but I was hoarding gestures,
the crinkle around your eyes, even
the dusky silence in the room,
survival harvest for the barren winters
when a wolf-wind would come howling
to sweep cruel through a house
bereft of us. So many winters gone
since that evening and, you know,
you were wrong. We don't forget
others, we only lose pieces
of ourselves. Your words, the tilt
of your head, even that silence
are still here, untouched.
It's the *me* who loved you,
the one I can't remember.

ELEGY

Sadder than the sadness
of losing you
is this tranquil knowing
you really didn't matter—
it goes deeper
than that
the primal flaw
that even love can't cure.
Hope is a rainbow
through a prism,
the deceiving
eye of the hurricane.
You or another failure
it would have been the same.

BLUE ELEGY

    I hate to see
your image
    (the evening sun)
disintegrate
    (go down)
leaving only the blue
blues of the evening,
specter of the rose
haunting the garden.

You were to be
my perfect grief,
the cleaving absence. I
mourn for my unbroken
heart singing in the
branches, the taste of
water you left, the
oblivious river closing
over you without a
trace, without a tear.

MARRONS GLACÉS

I hated them, these masterpieces
of confectionary art, bloated
in syrup baths, which would appear
in pastry shops when the first fogs
saddened our autumn. Plump and sleek
pampered odalisques on satin drapes,
they spilled from treasure chests,
piled high in shiny copper cauldrons,
a pyramid adorned with crystallized
violets, the purple petals candied in mid-
beat like tiny, imprisoned butterflies.
In the mouth, they melded to a cloying
paste that stuck to the palate, over-
whelmed taste buds, sent the pancreas
into overdrive. Even gluttons couldn't
eat more than two.

I loved chestnuts, the first, tiny
mountain ones charred over open flame
up at the lake, when late September rain
needled the window, knelled the death
of summer, the return to city and school.
With fingers, tongue turned black by soot,
I would suck the hard kernels, then bite
into a sudden floury sweetness, tinged
with smoke and charcoal—homey,
almost consoling: life would yield
simple answers, and be good.

In town, November brought the bigger
roasted chestnuts, smiling golden

from a slit in the shell. Wrapped
in a newspaper cone they warmed my hands
as I walked home from school in the grey-
red evenings of Milan still torn by war,
the fog like a veil over the silent
eviscerated houses. The belief in simple
answers long gone, but the "caldarroste"
plain and substantial, assuaged hunger
like a kept promise. Their scent erased
the acrid smell of other fires. Those
effete marrons glacés, returning safe
in their gilded boxes now seemed alien,
strangers who had not known those flames.

Now they're just part of the story,
Proustian capsules where a ten year-
old walks in a war-torn city lost in fog.
Still too sweet, but I have learned
to accept artifice. And, oh, those tiny,
candied violets…

In Italy, "Luna Parks" was the generic name given to itinerant amusement parks. The English name came, it seems, from a Victorian one in London.

LUNA PARKS

The story is always written
by the survivors, who can only tell
what didn't happen to them, the negative's
reversed space. I was not one of those
children machine-gunned near a carousel,
that's all I know. But forgotten evil
lives on to sink into a heavy void
that maims, and you don't know it.

They would appear in winter,
those Luna Parks, alighting in grey
snowy streets like rainbow-plumed
exotic birds. As a tinny calliope sang
a magic island bloomed out of the fog,
klieg lights sizzled white, raucous
dream barkers rasped their sirens' call.

Suddenly you believed in miracles,
in a world where men ate fire,
swallowed swords, shattered chains
taut around tattooed chest, walked
a blade of hand-to-mouth existence
unscathed. No one knew the ruins

soon to come in bombed houses,
the dead soldiers snared in barbed wire
in the snow, the icy wound
that kills the heartwood
while the leaves still grow.

They were such homey, gentle freaks:
the Fat Lady, smiling in immense deep-
chinned benevolence at the Monkey Boy
as she knitted a green shawl, the Tattooed
Man, with blue cobras writhing on his biceps
but "Mama" curlicued over his heart—
his baby asleep by the caravan.

How far away were the horrors of American
side shows, the phocomelic Seal Boy, the Living
Torso wrapped in a mink stole, her mother by her
side, images that would ambush you at night
in the mind's darkest streets: it could
be you, it is you, who but a freak
would pay to look at us? Those betraying
quick glances, the recoil in the gut
that denies kinship--and reveals it.

We were like children asleep while
a dam breaks. Our screams only
knew joy, as we asked for just one
more turn on the Whip, one last ride
on the roller coaster's waves,

a final swell that would spew us out
weak at the knees and laughing.

The Luna Parks are gone, forgotten
with those bombed houses, but the side
show remains. The freaks' dark parade
goes on, children with chopped-off arms
join the Seal Boy, the Tattooed Man
goes to a gas chamber with a blue
number on his wrist. And still
the calliope's tinny whine keeps on,
the grooved futility of that carousel
turns and turns to nowhere. On the wire
thin acrobats perform for a blind god.

FLY FISHING—LAKE COMO

My father is fly-casting
at the lake. A snap—the line
whips out graceful and cruel
over still water, a hand-tied lure
dances yellow and red
and weightless, a bright
nasturtium death. "It's all
in the wrist," he explains
as he pulls in a writhing pike,
a skill built on physics
and patience. My father opens
his creel, drops the pike
on a bed of grape leaves.
For a moment he's still, a dark figure
carving the morning's clarity.

At fifty-seven, he's flown planes
in two wars, escaped
from a prisoner's train
and now builds bridges
and loves fishing—and opera.
"*O patria mia*" he whistles softly
as he casts out, "*mai più, mai più...*"
The line snaps taut—a speckled trout,
this time. The creel's trap door opens
again to the green crypt. Aida joins
Radames in a living grave.

Around the lake September
has turned scarlet the woodbine,

empurpled grapes for the harvest. In
his harvest years, my father harvests
his lake. He doesn't know he too is
caught, the hook
invisible but deep. There'll be
no more Septembers. "*Il sogno*
é dileguato," my father hums.

Mai piú, mai piú." Inside the creel
the fish lie quiet in their leafy shroud.

MALLORQUIN

How generous
of this fig tree
that owes me nothing
to hide me from the road,
leaves like webbed hands
hold sunshine
and promises of fruit.
Shadowy patterns
vein my skin with green
filigree. Under
this living tent
Bedouin thoughts
come to rest. August
bleaches the shore.
Through my eyelashes
the sea, hit by the sun
explodes, eyes
drown in light.
Your image fades
to an over-exposed
photograph, edges
no longer cut. Under
the olive trees
a wandering
belled sheep
adds Syracusan
overtones, memories
of sleeping gods,
golden bees.

MONTEROSSO

Cinque Terre

I

Here where mountains descend,
rock to rock, into a sea
today so quiet, so gray
under the soundless rain
of a precocious September
that it evokes a confluence
of seasons come and gone
and the people you met
along the way (the path
at times easy, at times
as scabrous as the trails
that tie these five villages)
here, today, you feel the past
return: those quiet waves
become time's metronome—and yours.

II

The sun brings back August
with an explosion
of bougainvilleas
against a stucco wall,
red and yellow begonias
fat in their clay pots, basil
on a window sill. Midday,
a man comes by on the beach
selling coconut wedges
in a zinc bucket. He surges
out of time gone, and again

you are a child, that coconut
cool and white as white marble
in your hand—fragment of a past
you thought lost, while
it just went on without you.

Then you know:
what you've been, ends here
at this liquid infinity
so unknowable
it mocks the chances
you still believe in.
You feel diminished
by all you've left undone,
and yet strangely forgiven.

III

The sea assaults the rocks
today, an indigo and white fury
lashes blind at scrubby tamarisks
clinging stubbornly to a cliff.
Defenseless lemon trees
tremble in the garden.

Up at the station,
a mournful train
answers the roaring waves
as it pulls away.

SCUBA

*Oui! Grande mer de delires douée,
Peau de panthère—*

-P. Valéry

Le Cimetière Marin

The canopy
of Valery's panther's skin,
a golden fleece
that kills the sun—
zebra skin, rather,
from below,
liquid weight
suspended
like the lead on my belt,
silence,
flicks of fins
and disappears, green
green black
to vanish into,
a thin lifeline of air
rushes skyward in panic
as it should:
temptation is strong here.

We glide newborn
in a lost continent
of winged stillness:
stingrays, barracudas—
coral branches
vibrate to a mute echo
of Triton's horn.
Boundaries between elements

dissolve, primordial silence
dissolves even
the click of the camera.
The roll of pictures
you took of me
showed nothing but green water.
Cameras
don't lie.

OCEAN CITY

The journey
ends here, where it began.

I

How shall we return to the sea
besmirched beyond the boardwalk
by sticky clouds of cotton candy,
T-shirts with "Maryland is for crabs"
stenciled across the chest, the sign
for Blue Horizon Motel insidious waves
licked to ruin last April, how
will we dare reclaim
the silence of the starfish
blood-red against the reef?
Yet our spoor glistens on the sand
—gills to lungs, fins to footprints.

II

Early morning, July, the beach
empty, newly-born. Only an outlaw
black Labrador, drenched and happy,
barks at sandpipers in the waves.
Debris washes in, cuneiform messages
from a cryptic tide. Fragmented
angel wings, bone-bleached driftwood,
broken beer bottles polished to topaz
carry the lesson of all destructions:
in the stilled
song of blue whales
our own end waits.

III

A tribal need brings us all
here, to the edge. Anointed
for a forgotten ritual of renewal
we mimic death, let the midday sun
place copper coins on our eyelids.
In voices eroded by the wind
language reverts, becomes the cry
of earthbound gull, saved—or doomed—
by a lost instinct.

IV

Forecast of storm, the boardwalk
battens its hatches. The sea is lead
lining a coffin, desolation
of funerals in the rain. The sky
presses down in silent judgement.
Then, the wind. Tatar waves
invade the shore, slam the pier,
suck abandoned umbrellas to their doom.
The sea unmasks, a liquid Dies Irae
calls back drowned sailors.

V

But in the aftermath a heartbeat tide
ebbs and flows in the blood,
the inner sea calls salt to salt,
brings back the deep, the lost
gills, fin limbs, the swaying

anemone heart. We know you again,
then: we're yours and exiled
forever, wayward castaways
lighting bonfires on a winter
beach, thin air harsh
to sponge lungs, the grit of sand
alien and cold under our new feet.

MEMORIAL DAY, CAPE MAY, 2007

The fog came in from the sea
last night, a silent invasion
conquered the beach, seeped
across the highway into the garden
and in the mist ghosts came back,
memories of other landings--Anzio,
Salerno, Omaha Beach. Revenant
names, empty and pale as shells
left on the wet sand by the tide.

This morning, flags are dimmed
by the fog, droop from balconies,
but grills are readied, picnics
planned. It's the first holiday
week-end at the beach, the sun
surely knows his duty. The past?
The past at times is like a serpent's
outgrown skin, something better shed
along the way. And maybe we need to
forget in order to go on. Then
a fog comes in, blurs the present
in ambiguous nostalgia for what was.

Still, it's a May morning, at Anzio
Roman children splash in the waves
with happy, first-summer feet. "We'll
stop them at the tide line," *il Duce*
had promised on the radio. Maybe
the dead look down and forgive all.

By noon the sun has burned the ghosts
from the sea. Yes, summer is coming,
let the cuckoo sing. Suddenly, a
phalanx of black Rolling Thunder
motorcycles roars by the prized
Victorian gingerbread, chrome flashes
sharp as a blade in the sun.
Muted blue and shell-pink,
the hydrangeas nod their heavy
balloon heads in the wind.

THE SHAPE OF WATER

(San Giovanni, Lake Como)

A lizard basks on red granite,
its tail a comma between last
and first name. I never knew
this Grandi, Roberto, whose tomb
the lizard is editing, but as I walk
gravel paths among the silent neighbors
of my grandparents' graves, faces,
names surge to greet me. Ginevra,
my grandmother's maid, who could dance
the charleston. Carlo, her carpenter
husband. Tomaso from the sweets shop,
who gave me a candy for each year
on my birthday. And Nino, tall
and thin, who rented boats
at the small harbor by our garden gate.

I recognized them all. But who
were they, these familiar strangers,
the adults of my childhood summers?
I count the decades of their lives
I never knew, carved deep on slabs
and all I hold are labile phantoms
of a past as fluid as this lake
so deceptively unchanged, so still
under the gold of a September sun,
while a river runs cold and unseen
in its depth--glaciers' ice and snow
melted by time, mutating like our lives.

KISMET

Yellow crocus
hiding your turban
among the dandelions,

slumming Caliph
roaming at night
Baghdad's seamy streets

in search of a true love,
take heed: fate
plays tricks with dreams.

You might be mistaken
for a weed, tossed
on the compost heap

while the princess
who loves you
waits in the palace

desolate and alone.

OF SAINTS AND SNOWS

The life-size St. Francis
preaching to pigeons,
bronze and real, at the fountain
in the square (the live ones
asleep, puffed up to ruffled
grey balls against the cold)
offered me a friendly blessing
with a hand filled with snow
as I snuck by to meet you.
That candid benediction
gave me hope. Surely
a saint who could tame a wolf
and cared for stupid pigeons
would find a way to rescue
an impossible love.

But we had such a bleak,
soul-searing winter that year,
and even an indulgent saint
can get weary, bare feet
in snow, snow furring his cowl,
trickling down to an emaciated
bronze chest. Perhaps I asked
too much, perhaps I should have
picked a sturdier savior. Now,

I know better. The open wounds
of youth become with time
bloodless and precious
as the bronze stigmata

hidden by that giving snow.
A few flakes in the air
and all comes back: you
and me, and Francis, forever
safe in an endless winter
bitter and sharp and perfect.

GOING BACK

My brain is cosmopolitan:
has traveled to Tibet,
shifts gears smoothly
between four languages,
goes to the opera, reads
Proust in the original,
enjoys fusion cuisine,
gravlax, brut champagne.
But recently my stomach
is turning peasant. It craves
the rustic fare of long-gone
Lombard autumns: polenta
yellow in a copper cauldron,
uncouth mountain cheese tasting
of whey, hot chestnuts swimming
in milk, green and purple figs
fresh from the tree and, like
a greedy child, looks forward
to the squat panettone of yester-
year, to a brittle, hard bar
of *torrone* for Christmas.
Perhaps there is a simple
animal wisdom here, in this
return to comforts one knew,
the acceptance of an ending cycle,
like the dead leaves going back
to earth under a silent
autumn rain, like the earth
preparing for the winter snows.

LETTER TO YANG CHEN CHAI

(1090-1138)

I thought you'd like to know how strong
the permanence of impermanence can be:
almost a thousand years and the footprints
you left with those blue slippers as you stepped
onto a ferry's landing slick with frost
endure. A morning at the Ta Kao gorge
so lost in fog you couldn't see the mountains
nor the river, and only a baying dog —probably
unhappy after a long night out in the cold—
and the crowing from an unseen rooster
helped guide you to the village. A thousand years

and I watch you step out of the page,
endearing traveler from another shore
with those bright blue, upbeat slippers.
And while I think of Charon and his boat,
of whom you knew nothing— any crossing
to an unseen land can feel the same,
doesn't it, in spite of time and different
fogs hiding the path—I have no need
for that unhappy dog nor that rooster,
not with your footprints etched so clear
in virgin frost, and a bright touch of blue.

OPERA BALL AT THE GERMAN EMBASSY

"I'm from Mallorca" the Spanish
ambassador tells me at dinner. Just
a name, and those long-gone summers
flow back unbidden in a golden tide:
amphibious days, the morning sea
like a second skin, smooth, essential,
the sun flaming the air to a mirage
of possibilities, a life outside time,
outside thought. Fringed afternoons
under a canopied fig tree, sharing
the honeyed fruit with drunken bees,
blackberries ripe along white dusty roads,
the scent of wild anise in the wind.
And always the sea, the immensely blue,
embracing sea. Strange how our years
become books we read only once
and store on a shelf. Then, a word,
and days fall out from a random page
like pressed flowers.

At the embassy, together with a table
carved out of ice—salmon sushi, clams—
they've built an eight-foot replica
of the Berlin wall, in celebration. Twenty
years since it came down. Plaster board
and rough stucco, splotchy red and black
graffiti. Ugly as the real thing, but no
bodies snared on barbed wire. People pose
in front of it, drinking champagne.

A woman admires my gown—perfect
for a summer ball.

Next morning, at the hospice. I change
the dressing on a patient. Cancer
has carved a jagged cave beneath
his jaw, strands of necrotic stalactites
hang down. Burl-knots of fresh tumors
cropped up along the neck, "My ear
feels blocked" he says. "It must
be wax." I nod. We keep no mirrors
at the hospice. I watch the carotid
pulsate exposed, reinforce the dressing.
"Yes," I say, "That wax can really
be a pain." Those Mallorcan days
fill the room. The wall stands there.

ABOUT THE AUTHOR

LAURA BRYLAWSKI-MILLER was born and raised in Milan, Italy, and as a small child during WWII experienced the devastating air raids on that city. Echoes of those events can be found in her poems. She was educated in Classic Humanities and always intended to be a fiction writer.

When she came to the U.S. upon her marriage, her English (which she had learned by reading Walt Disney's comic books) was inadequate for any meaningful writing, so she turned to painting, studied gemology and concentrated on family matters. A fortuitous series of events resulted in an interest in medicine as well as a re-awakened need to write. She obtained a Bachelor of Science in Health Sciences from the Physician's Assistant program at George Washington University, and worked for years as a surgical resident at a local hospital as well as volunteering at the acute care facility of a Virginia hospice and the Arlington Free Clinic. She also received an MFA in Creative Writing from The American University.

Her publications include three poetry collection and three novels, as well as essays and medical articles.

She lives in Arlington, VA, and travels frequently between the U.S. and Italy. She has forgotten most of the Latin and Ancient Greek of her youth, but besides Italian and English, she is fluent in French and Spanish.

www.ingramcontent.com/pod-product-compliance
Lightning Source LLC
Chambersburg PA
CBHW021128300426
44113CB00006B/335